AR 3.6
pts 0.5

D0742951

Bears

Therese Shea

press

New York

Published in 2007 by The Rosen Publishing Group, Inc.
29 East 21st Street, New York, NY 10010

Book Design: Michael J. Flynn

Photo Credits: Cover, p. 15 © Roman Krochuk/Shutterstock; p. 5 © George Lee/Shutterstock; p. 7 © Ian Scott/Shutterstock; p. 9 © Michael Thompson/Shutterstock; p. 11 © Patrick Rolands/Shutterstock; p. 13 © Jacqueline Shaw/Shutterstock; p. 17 © Daniel Hebert/Shutterstock; p. 19 © Keith Levit/Shutterstock; p. 21 © Oliver Suckling/Shutterstock; p. 22 © Vladimir Pomortzeff/Shutterstock.

Library of Congress Cataloging-in-Publication Data

Shea, Therese.
  Bears / Therese Shea.
      p. cm. — (Big bad biters)
  Includes index.
  ISBN-13: 978-1-4042-3524-8
  ISBN-10: 1-4042-3524-8 (library binding)
  1. Bears—Juvenile literature. I. Title. II. Series: Shea, Therese. Big bad biters.
  QL737.C27S4754 2007
  599.78—dc22
                                2006015118

Manufactured in the United States of America

Contents

Bears Everywhere!

Small and cuddly. Big and scary. Long claws. Soft fur. Sharp teeth. All of these words describe bears. You probably have seen cartoon bears on television. Bears are characters in many children's books. Maybe you have even seen a real bear in a zoo. Bears are almost everywhere you look!

Wild bears live in North America, Asia, Europe, and around the North Pole. One kind of bear lives in South America. Let's learn about bears and their big bad bite!

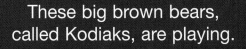

These big brown bears, called Kodiaks, are playing.

5

Short Legs, Sharp Claws

All bears have thick fur and large heads with small eyes and small, round ears. They have short, strong legs. Bears can walk upright, like people, on two big feet. A large bear can have feet that are 16 inches (41 cm) long! Each foot has five toes, and each toe has one long claw. Bears use their claws to find food or attack **prey**.

Bears look like they might be slow because they have short legs and large feet. However, some kinds can move very quickly.

Polar bears can run as fast as 35 miles (56 km) an hour and swim as fast as 6 miles (10 km) an hour.

Finding Food

Bears eat mostly meat. They hunt for fish, mice, squirrels, ants, eggs, **grubs**, and small forest animals. Bears also eat fruit berries, nuts, and leaves. They can tear apart beehives to get honey. Their thick fur keeps them safe from bee stings.

Some bears travel far to find food. Polar bears have been found more than 200 miles (322 km) from land on floating ice. Hungry grizzlies may roam over an area as large as 12 square miles (31 sq km) in search of food.

Bears' sense of smell helps them find food. This bear caught a fish with its teeth.

9

Sleeping Through Winter

Bears mostly live and hunt alone. Some bears eat large amounts of food in summer to get ready for winter. They go into a **den** when it gets cold outside. A den may be a cave, a pile of sticks, or a hole dug under a tree. A bear may spend most of winter sleeping in its den. Some scientists call the bear's sleep **hibernation**. Others think bears do not really hibernate because they sometimes wake up and go outside on warm winter days.

Most brown bears, like the one shown here, sleep through winter. Most polar bears stay active throughout winter.

Bear Cubs

Bears **mate** during the summer. A female bear may give birth to one to four cubs during the winter. Cubs usually weigh less than 1 pound (454 g). They are born without fur and with their eyes closed. A month later, cubs have soft fur and can open their eyes. They go outside the den for the first time in spring. Some cubs stay with their mother for up to $3\frac{1}{2}$ years. She teaches them to hunt during this time.

Bear cubs like to play with each other.

13

Big Brown Bears

Big brown bears live in Asia, Europe, and North America. They can be many colors.

Some brown bears in northwestern North America are called grizzly bears. Grizzlies have brown or black fur with white-tipped hairs. Full-grown grizzlies can be 8 feet (2.4 m) long. Male grizzlies can weigh up to 1,500 pounds (681 kg). Grizzlies use their jaws to grab fish out of the water. They can eat up to 90 pounds (41 kg) of food a day, including large animals such as moose.

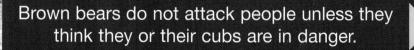

Brown bears do not attack people unless they think they or their cubs are in danger.

American Black Bears

The most common bear in North America is the American black bear. They grow 5 feet (1.5 m) long and usually weigh up to 300 pounds (136 kg). Black bears can actually be different colors. One kind of black bear has gray and black fur that makes it look blue!

Black bears may bite into a fallen log to eat the ants living inside. They also like eating hard-shelled **hickory** nuts. A person would need a hammer to open this kind of nut!

Black bears are good climbers. Some make winter dens in hollow trees up to 100 feet (30 m) off the ground!

Polar Bears

Polar bears live near the North Pole. Male polar bears can be over 11 feet (3.4 m) tall and weigh over 1,000 pounds (454 kg)! Polar bears have very thick white fur. This keeps them warm in the icy water.

Polar bears can smell food from 10 miles (16 km) away! They mostly eat sea animals, such as fish, walruses, and seals. Their teeth are sharper than other bears' teeth since they eat more meat and fewer plants.

Polar bears may wait near a hole in the ice that a seal uses to breathe. When the seal comes up for air, the polar bear grabs it with its teeth!

Bears in Danger

A few kinds of bears have come close to dying out. Throughout history, people have hunted bears for meat, fur, or just for fun. Bears have lost much of their forest homes as people build on their land. Also, **global warming** may be causing polar bears to lose their icy hunting grounds. We must learn more about how to help bears continue to exist in our world.

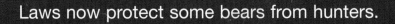

Laws now protect some bears from hunters.

More Kinds of Bears

We have learned about big brown bears, American black bears, and polar bears. There are many other kinds of bears. Asiatic black bears have a moon-shaped white mark on their chest. Some think their meat and bones have healing powers. Sun bears are the smallest bears. They can open coconuts with their teeth! Sloth bears move slowly and make loud noises. One kind of South American bear has marks around its eyes that look like glasses. Bears may seem scary, but they are fun to learn about!

Glossary

den (DEHN) The shelter or resting place of a wild animal.

global warming (GLOH-buhl WOHR-ming) An increase in the warmth of the air surrounding Earth, which may be caused in part by people burning some kinds of fuel.

grub (GRUB) A soft, thick, wormlike animal.

hibernation (hy-bur-NAY-shun) The act of passing the winter in a resting state.

hickory (HIH-kuh-ree) A tall tree that has tough wood and produces a nut in a hard shell.

mate (MAYT) When a male and a female join to make babies.

prey (PRAY) An animal that is hunted by another animal as food.

Index

A
American black bear(s), 16, 22
Asia, 4, 14
Asiatic black bears, 22

B
big brown bears, 14, 22

C
claw(s), 4, 6
cubs, 12

D
den, 10, 12
dying out, 20

E
ears, 6
eat(ing), 8, 10, 14, 16, 18
Europe, 4, 14
eyes, 6, 12, 22

F
food, 8, 10, 14, 18
foot (feet), 6
fur, 4, 6, 8, 12, 14, 16, 18, 20

G
global warming, 20
grizzlies, 8, 14

H
hibernate(ion), 10
hunt(ed), 8, 10, 12, 20

L
legs, 6

M
mate, 12

N
North America, 4, 14, 16
North Pole, 4, 18

P
polar bears, 8, 18, 20, 22
prey, 6

S
sloth bears, 22
South America(n), 4, 22
sun bears, 22

T
teeth, 4, 18, 22

W
walk upright, 6

Web Sites

Due to the changing nature of Internet links, PowerKids Press has developed an online list of Web sites related to the subject of this book. This site is updated regularly. Please use this link to access the list:
http://www.powerkidslinks.com/biters/bears/